Original title:
Carols and Cinnamon

Copyright © 2024 Creative Arts Management OÜ
All rights reserved.

Author: Victor Mercer
ISBN HARDBACK: 978-9916-90-952-2
ISBN PAPERBACK: 978-9916-90-953-9

Savoring the Chill with a Warm Heart

When winter winds are blowing cold,
We wrap ourselves in scarves of bold.
A cup of cocoa in our hand,
We dream of beaches, sun, and sand.

The snowflakes fall with frosty glee,
But hot cocoa's our jubilee.
We sip and slurp, it's all a game,
While plotting how to stay the same.

The biting chill can't touch our pride,
In fluffy slippers, we do glide.
With every shiver, we just grin,
For winter's fun is about to begin.

So raise your mugs and shout a cheer,
For winter nights we hold so dear!
With warmth inside, let laughter flow,
Savor the chill, let good times grow!

Wrapped in Warmth and Melody

In cozy socks, we prance around,
The cat's our DJ, spinning sound.
Hot cocoa flows like melted dreams,
As marshmallows drench our silly schemes.

We dance like penguins in the night,
With every sip, we lose our fright.
Wrapped in blankets, we take flight,
While laughter fills the frosty light.

Mirth in Every Sip

Grab your cup, it's time to cheer,
With every sip, we lose our fear.
Coffee's hotter than our wildest hopes,
And tea is brewing giggly scopes.

Let's toast to life, the quirky bits,
With smoothies made from life's weird tricks.
We laugh and spill, oh what a scene,
In each warm drink, joy is the queen.

Solstice Nights and Tasty Bites

On solstice nights, the fire's bright,
We munch on snacks, oh what a sight!
Cookies crumble, chips take flight,
As laughter dances in the night.

The punch is potent, let's not lie,
It makes us sing and reach for the sky.
With every bite and every cheer,
We'll celebrate, our fun is here!

Nestled Under Twinkling Stars

Under stars that wink and glow,
We tell tall tales of things we know.
Campfire smoke wraps us like a hug,
As stardust tickles our tired mug.

S'mores are melting, gooey and bright,
While fireflies join our gleeful flight.
With sleepy eyes and silly grins,
The night enchants as laughter spins.

Frosted Mornings

The coffee spills, I slip and slide,
My breakfast taco's gone to hide.
A frosted window, icy glare,
I can't feel toes, why do I care?

Spiced Dreams

Last night I dreamt of gingerbread,
But woke to find it all in my head.
Cinnamon swirls in the morning air,
My cat's got a whisker in her hair.

The Tune of Toasted Nuts

Almonds sing from the toaster's grip,
While walnuts dance, and hazelnuts flip.
A symphony of crunch in this pot,
If only the squirrels would share a lot!

Holiday Hearth and Harmony

The fire's crackling, tales unfold,
But Uncle Joe's jokes never get old.
With cookies stacked like a snowy hill,
We laugh till our cheeks feel the chill.

Echoes Through the Frosted Pines

A snowman's hat is slightly askew,
He's judging me for what I chew.
With pinecone wishes floating around,
I hope my snacks won't soon be found.

Aroma of Gathered Hearts

The kitchen's a circus, ingredients fly,
Moms whisking like wizards, oh my, oh my!
Cookies are dancing, flour's taking flight,
Can't find the cake? It's hidden from sight.

Uncles are fighting for the last piece of pie,
Auntie's on Twitter, not knowing why.
Laughter erupts like a pot on the stove,
In this glorious chaos, we all feel the love.

Threads of Festive Light

Twinkling lights wrapped around the cat,
He's more than a decoration, imagine that!
The tree's leaning sideways, it needs a strong coat,
Not sure if it's art or a dramatic flat boat.

Grandpa's on the roof, but has lost his way,
Yelling for help but it's all in dismay.
With ornaments falling, it's a sight quite surreal,
Our holiday spirit? It's a wonderful deal.

Whispers of Winter Nights

Snowflakes are falling, it's chilly and bright,
Kids in their pajamas, oh what a sight!
Hot cocoa spills over, marshmallows afloat,
Mom's looking for towels, we'll need them to gloat.

The snowman has moaned, arms made of sticks,
He's planning a party, here come the tricks!
The laughter of children, like bells in the night,
Whispers and giggles, it feels just right.

Sugar Spice Serenade

In grandma's kitchen, we mix up a tune,
Whisking and stirring, oh how they swoon!
Sugar and spice, a dash of delight,
Confections so sweet, make teeth feel the fright.

Sprinkles are flying, like confetti in air,
Last year's leftovers? Who really would dare?
Baking disasters, we laugh and we cry,
In our sugar spice life, we let out a sigh.

Evening Lights and Sugared Delights

The sun dips low, the stars take flight,
A chocolate cake, just out of sight.
With sprinkles dancing on my nose,
I laugh at how the icing glows.

Candles flicker, shadows prance,
Join my silly, sweetened dance.
Spritz of lemon, a dash of fun,
In this kitchen, I'm number one!

Giggling cookies, oh what a sight,
Doughy hands in pure delight.
Whisking fluff like a crazy chef,
Who needs perfection? Not this ref!

So raise your spoon, let's take a bite,
Life's too short, let's end this night.
With evening lights, and sugar rush,
In this sweet, dessert-filled hush.

The Dance of Citrus and Clove

Citrus fruits in a wobbly bowl,
Twist and twirl, what a joyful stroll!
Clove whispers hints of holiday cheer,
Let's dance in zest, the season is here!

Lemons leap and oranges roll,
Twirling around like they're on patrol.
Ginger snaps with quirky flair,
Spicy moves in the cool night air.

Lime and tangerine join the fray,
Spinning wildly 'til they sway.
Join the beat of their zestful tune,
Underneath the glimmering moon.

In this merry fruitball, we'll shine,
Sipping punch, feeling divine.
So grab a fruit, escape your woes,
In this dance of citrus and cloves.

Savoring Moments Beneath the Boughs

Underneath the leafy crown,
Sips of nectar from the town.
Honey drips, oh what a treat,
Life is grand in summer's heat!

Picnic blankets, ants in a line,
Chasing crumbs? They sure dine fine!
Beneath the boughs, stories unfold,
As laughter sparkles like marigold.

Watermelon slices, oh so neat,
Juicy tales that can't be beat.
With laughter ringing through the trees,
Nature's stage, aim to please!

So let's toast to this blissful hour,
Underneath our leafy bower.
Savoring those moments so sweet,
Time rolls on, but we can't be beat!

Lullabies in Sweaters

Snug in warmth, our sweaters hum,
The world outside begins to numb.
Hot cocoa whispers sweet goodnight,
As cozy dreams take their flight.

Mismatched socks, a giggle fest,
Chasing shadows, never rest.
Tangled blankets, a quilted maze,
In this chaos, we find our praise.

Lullabies spoken in playful rhymes,
Drift into dreams, oh how the time climbs.
Each stitch woven with love so tight,
We rock and sway till morning light.

So here's to sweaters, laughter, and cheer,
Our winter wonderland, oh so dear.
With lullabies soft, the night's embrace,
In this warm hug, we find our place.

Twinkling Lights and Spices Bright

Twinkling lights on every tree,
Chasing cats, oh what a spree!
Gingerbread men run away fast,
Too sweet to let them stay past.

Cookies burn, oh what a fright,
Forgot them in the oven's bite.
Sprinkle sugar on my hair,
Holiday cheer, I can't help but wear!

Stockings hung with a big old grin,
Grumpy uncle's dance is a win!
Eggnog spills from my new shirt,
At this party, I'm the dessert!

Twinkling lights come out to play,
Spiced chaos, yay, hooray!
Holiday laughter fills the night,
With twinkling lights, we're all feeling bright!

Songs of the Season's Embrace

Jingle bells ringing off tune,
Neighbors hiding, hoping it's noon.
Out of tune, our choir's a sight,
Caroling with pure delight!

Silent night turns into a show,
Grandma's voice can really blow!
But the cat's now in the bass,
Singing loud with a furry face.

Frosty's got moves, oh what a guy,
Dancing in the backyard, oh my!
With a snowman doing the twist,
It's the party you can't miss!

Songs of laughter fill the air,
With off-key notes, who really cares?
Grab a mug of hot cocoa near,
Join the chorus, spread the cheer!

Scented Memories of Yule

Cinnamon swirls and nutmeg dreams,
Burning candles, or so it seems.
Scented memories fill the room,
Like Aunt Mildred's famous mushroom!

Eggnog mixed with a pinch of cheer,
Lurking onions, what a fear!
Apple pie on the kitchen floor,
The pet dog thinks it's a score!

Oranges poked with cloves around,
Cherished gifts we all have found.
Wrapped up tight with shiny bows,
Maybe twice, they'll go on toes!

Scented memories, never old,
Each whiff a tale waiting to unfold.
With laughter and joy, we sing and play,
Let's keep these scents around each day!

Warmth Wrapped in Melody

Huddled close by the fireplace glow,
Blankets wrapped tight, like a cozy show.
Hot cocoa sips and a wink of delight,
Singing silly songs deep into the night!

Pajamas with reindeer, they dance and prance,
Grandpa attempts a wild, goofy dance.
Laughter erupts, it's quite the scene,
As Uncle Joe does the splits, so keen!

Snowflakes swirl outside our door,
Kids in the yard want to explore.
Warmth of laughter and hugs galore,
Joyful hearts, who could ask for more?

Wrapped in melody, we celebrate,
Memories made, oh it's never too late.
In this warmth, we shall always stay,
Creating magic in every way!

Glimmers of Joy and Spice

In the kitchen, pots do dance,
With ginger and nutmeg, here's your chance.
The cookies burn, oh what a sight,
But we'll eat them anyway, if we bite!

Laughter echoes, spices flare,
A sprinkle of joy hangs in the air.
Frosting fights, and dough takes flight,
The chaos brings us pure delight!

With flavors mixed like friends we share,
Waiting for miracles, unaware.
Together in mess, we laugh and chime,
Creating memories, one crumb at a time!

Candied Voices in the Snow

Snowflakes fall like candy sweet,
We bundle up in woolen fleet.
Sledding down the icy hill,
We giggle, tumble, scream – what a thrill!

Voices blend like sugar spun,
Making memories, oh what fun!
A snowman croaks with a carrot nose,
While we toss snowballs, in warm clothes!

Hot cocoa spills, marshmallows fly,
Our laughter fills the chilly sky.
Candied voices in winter's glow,
Chasing away the clouds of woe!

Joyous Gatherings by the Fire

Flames leap high in the cozy den,
With stories spun 'round again and again.
S'mores are crafted, oh so divine,
But someone's burnt them – oh, never mind!

Friends gather close, sharing a laugh,
We take silly photos, do the math.
The dog steals the snacks when we're not aware,
Yet this chaos makes it more rare!

Warmth surrounds us, united in cheer,
As we recount memories from the year.
Loud voices drown out the crackling fire,
Only joy can take us higher!

The Scent of Celebration

The oven puffs with aromas bright,
As we dance 'round the kitchen, sheer delight.
Spices twirl and flavors boast,
Whipped cream flying, we toast the most!

Music plays while we roast the nuts,
Spilling drinks – oh, look at those guts!
Everyone sings, even the cat —
Who thought a party looked like that?

Cheers ripple through the festive night,
From sugary treats to laughter's height.
The scent of celebration fills the room,
With joy exploding, it's sure to bloom!

The Aroma of Togetherness

In the kitchen, chaos reigns,
Cookies burn, but who complains?
Flouring the cat, we giggle loud,
Never thought we'd be this proud.

Mom's recipe, we try to tweak,
Adding chocolate, oh so sleek.
Dad steals bites, with mischief bold,
Our secret's out, the truth is told.

Flour fights and laughter shared,
No one's mad, we're unprepared.
In this mess, we find our bliss,
Togetherness tastes like chocolate kiss.

From burnt cuisine to silly games,
We cherish all, despite our claims.
Through blunders, joy finds its place,
In every smile, a warm embrace.

Twinkling Lights and Laughter

Stringing lights, we make a scene,
Tripping over cords, it's quite routine.
"Watch the ladder!" someone shouts,
While tangled up in Christmas sprouts.

Hot cocoa spills, we laugh it off,
As kids dance round, our spirits scoff.
Mistletoe hung, we run away,
Who knew love could be this cliché?

The tree leans like it's had a drink,
Or maybe it's just time to rethink.
Lights flicker, and the cat takes charge,
In this chaos, we feel so large.

"More cookies!" someone starts to chant,
But Auntie's voice rises, "Only plant!"
With twinkling lights and laughter bright,
We welcome winter's joyful night.

A Bitter-Sweet Symphony

Life's like chocolate, bittersweet,
A surprise in every treat.
We dance through highs, we stumble low,
Laughing at all the chaos flow.

Meetings drags, what's on the clock?
Bob brings donuts, oh, what a shock!
Sweeten the deal, pretend to work,
While visions of treats begin to lurk.

The music plays, we sing off-key,
Dance on the table, just you and me.
The highs and lows, they intertwine,
In every moment, a little divine.

So raise your cup, let's toast this ride,
With bitter steps on this joy-filled tide.
We've found our way through laughter's grace,
In this symphony, we've found our place.

Memories Stirred with Spice

In grandmas pot, the aromas swell,
Ginger and garlic, we can't quite tell.
A pinch of memories, a stir of cheer,
Every sprinkle brings laughter near.

Sautéing onions, oh what a tear,
Crying for meals made with care.
"Is that the spice or your bad joke?"
With every laugh, the love awoke.

In the corner, the kids play hide,
Nutmeg escapes, it's time to bide.
Laughter's seasoning, it's clear to see,
In every taste, sweet memory.

So gather 'round, let's feast today,
For spiced moments never fade away.
Through every meal, we share our hearts,
In memories stirred, the laughter starts.

In the Glow of Holiday Cheer

The tree's up high, lights all aglow,
Cats are scaling, oh what a show.
Cookies are baking, they smell divine,
But I just dropped one—now it's mine!

Uncle Bob's dancing, a sight to behold,
With moves so wild, and no shame at all.
The eggnog's flowing, laughter's loud,
Family around me, I feel so proud.

Aunt Sue's in the kitchen, stirring away,
She claims it's magic, but we just say,
Her secret's the wine, we all know the score,
She adds a splash more and says, "Just one more!"

As holiday songs fill the chilly air,
We sing off-key without a care.
In this glow, we forget all our fears,
And toast to joy, with laughter and cheers!

Dancing Shadows and Spiced Lullabies

Shadows are dancing on the wall,
With spooky stories, we all enthrall.
The candles flicker, creating a fright,
Even the cat is hidden from sight!

Spiced pumpkin pie rests on the tray,
But it's Aunt May who'll eat it all day.
With whispers of ghosts, we giggle in fright,
While someone laughs loud, it's quite a sight!

The kids play dodge, with giggles and screams,
Imagining monsters, as wild as dreams.
Each spiced lullaby hums through the night,
Till we drift away, in pure delight.

So here's to the shadows that creep and sway,
And the joy that visits each Halloween play.
With laughter and love, our hearts will fly,
As we cherish the moments, just you and I!

Echoes of Togetherness

Around the dinner table, we gather near,
With favorite dishes and holiday cheer.
Dad's telling stories, with his classic flair,
While Grandma's recipes fill up the air.

Sisters are bickering, but it's all in fun,
While the brother sneaks cookies—has he begun?
A game of charades brings laughter so bright,
As we act like penguins, to the family's delight!

The crackling fire, a cozy retreat,
Uncle Joe's snoring, he's lost to the beat.
Each echo of laughter fills up the room,
In this warm gathering, joy will bloom.

So here's to togetherness, loud and bold,
In moments like these, love is our gold.
With heartwarming tales and a dash of cheer,
We'll treasure the echoes that draw us near!

Memory Lane Wrapped in Flavors

Down memory lane, with flavors so bright,
Home-made dishes bring pure delight.
Mom's chili bubbling, a family fave,
Dad's cornbread rising, it's the taste we crave.

Each grain of rice holds a story or two,
As we laugh about spills and the pranks that we do.
With every bite, our memories swirl,
Around the dining table, watch the joy unfurl!

The recipes whispered in the kitchen's warm glow,
Passed down with laughter, like an old friend's show.
From savory pastries to sweet apple pies,
The flavors of home hold the biggest surprise.

So let's feast together, from dish to dish,
Drowning in flavors, fulfilling each wish.
With moments made tasty, we linger and stay,
On this memory lane, we'll savor each day!

Chants of the Frosted Moon

The moon hangs high, a frozen pie,
Squirrels in coats, they scamper by.
They chant of snowflakes, oh what a scene,
While penguins waddle, looking quite keen.

Snowmen at night have a snowball fight,
With carrots for noses, they're quite a sight.
But when dawn breaks, their giggles fade,
Oh frosted moon, where's the fun we made?

Icicles dangle, like teeth of a beast,
Challenging snowflakes to a chilly feast.
But they melt away in a sunny glow,
Leaving just puddles, where did they go?

So here's to the frost, and the laughter it brings,
With cheeky jokes that the winter sings.
In the icy air, we dance and prance,
With frosted moonlight, we'll take our chance.

The Invitation of Warmth

A knock on the door, who could that be?
It's grandma with cookies and so much glee.
With mittens she offers, a warm embrace,
The smell of cinnamon, oh what a place!

The fireplace crackles, a festive song,
As the cat steals a seat, where it belongs.
We gather 'round, spirits feeling bright,
Mugs of hot cocoa, a sweet delight!

Let's dance like fools, in our fuzzy socks,
And sing to the moon, while the clock still tocks.
The warmth of our laughter fills up the room,
Inviting more joy, pushing away gloom.

So here's to the hugs and cozy nights,
Where roasted marshmallows reach new heights.
With hearts so full and grins that gleam,
Life is but a warm, delicious dream!

Gingered Whispers of Nostalgia

In a kitchen so warm, the scents arise,
Gingerbread men dance, oh how they surprise!
With frosting for smiles and gumdrops for eyes,
They whisper sweet tales under sugar skies.

Old recipe books, with edges worn thin,
Each page holds a memory, where to begin?
Flour fights at noon, it's a family rite,
In the battle of cookies, we laugh and bite!

Spicing up tales of yesteryear,
With nutmeg and laughter, we gather near.
The warmth in our hearts, gingered and bright,
In nostalgia's hug, all feels just right.

So let's bake some joy, with love as our guide,
In a world filled with sugar, we'll take it in stride.
For every cookie tells a story unique,
In gingered whispers, the past we seek!

Wrapped in Twinkling Dreams

Under a blanket of shimmering stars,
We toast with hot chocolate, forget all the wars.
The twinkling lights, oh, what a sight,
Each bulb a wish, glowing so bright!

With laughter and stories, we gather 'round,
While Santa's just down the street, safe and sound.
He's checking his list, with a quirk in his eye,
Making sure naughty kids don't just say goodbye!

Snowflakes descend, like confetti in air,
Each one a secret, a mystery to share.
We wrap up our dreams, like gifts to behold,
With ribbons and sparkles, tales yet untold.

So here's to the nights of whimsical cheer,
Where magic and wishes come true every year.
Wrapped in twinkling dreams, let's dance and sing,
Merry moments like jewels, let the joy ring!

Sweet Notes of a Winter's Eve

The snowflakes dance in twirls so bright,
While hot cocoa spills, oh what a sight!
My cat wears a scarf, looking so grand,
As it paws at the snow, softening the land.

Outside trees shimmer, bless their bright lights,
While inside I munch on holiday bites.
The turkey's still dancing, can you believe?
It's the sweet notes of a winter's eve!

Grandma's knitting socks, but missed the stitches,
My grandpa just snores, oh what a glitch!
With each little mishap, we laugh out loud,
Creating sweet moments that make us so proud.

So gather around with joy and cheer,
Let's raise a mug filled with holiday beer!
For in this cozy, warm fest we weave,
Only sweet notes of a winter's eve!

Buttered Rum and Harmony

On a chilly night, we gather near,
With buttered rum, we toast and cheer.
Each swig warms up our tummies bright,
While the cat purrs softly, such pure delight.

The cookies burn, what a hilarious flop!
But we munch on the edges, zest in each drop.
With laughter and giggles, we sing a song,
Creating a harmony that can't be wrong.

Grandma spins yarns, tales wilder than dreams,
While uncles just nod, lost in their creams.
The dog steals a sip, oh such a delight,
As we jive in the warmth of this magical night.

So let's sip and sway, let the joy swirl,
With buttered rum flowing, let laughter unfurl!
Through festive mishaps, so plenty and free,
We find our sweet harmony, just you and me!

Whirls of Cinnamon Whispers

In the kitchen, a scent fills the air,
Cinnamon swirls—oh, not a care!
My dog in a hat, so snug and so nice,
While he stares at the cookies like they're paradise.

Stirring the batter, I drop in a shoe,
Not my best move, but hey, who knew?
With flour on faces, and laughs that won't quit,
We bake up a storm, this madness is it!

So come grab a seat, and please watch your seat,
As the gingerbread men dance on our feet.
Each nibble brings giggles, each sip brings delight,
Whirls of cinnamon whispers make everything right.

We'll sing with the spoons and laugh till we drop,
This riot of flavors? Why, it just won't stop!
As long as we're here, forever we'll grin,
In our kitchen of mistakes, let the fun begin!

Frost-kissed Melodies

With frost on the windows, the world turns white,
While we bundle up warm, snug through the night.
Outside is a wonderland, pure and divine,
As we dance in our socks, feel the chill in our spine.

The snowman we built? Well, he lost his hat,
Now he's balding and super fat!
We laugh as we toss snowballs in the air,
While the neighbor yells, "Watch out! Be fair!"

Frost-kissed melodies hum through the trees,
While we sip on some tea, feeling quite at ease.
Each giggle and gig, each joyful cheer,
Turns this winter's night into one we hold dear.

So let's keep on dancing through frost and the fun,
With a sleigh full of laughter, the night's just begun.
For the memories we make, in situations precise,
Becomes our frost-kissed song, a loving device!

Hearthside Harmonies

By the fire, the marshmallows toast,
We sing silly songs, each one a boast.
Uncle Joe croons, it's quite a sight,
While Aunt May squeaks, her voice takes flight.

The dog joins in, with a woof and a howl,
As the cat gives a look, as if to scowl.
In this cozy chaos, laughter spills,
Who knew a tune could give such thrills?

Grandma's knitting, catching the beat,
Her yarn is a mess, but it's quite the treat.
The clock strikes seven, our voices grow,
As we harmonize, to the fire's glow.

With cocoa in hand, we all raise a cheer,
More hugs, less fuss, and a sprinkle of cheer.
"Come join us!" we call, to every pet,
This hearthside harmony, we won't forget!

Boughs of Evergreen Verse

In the living room, stands our grand tree,
A boughs of green, just as jolly as can be.
With ornaments dangling, a few cats too,
They think it's a jungle, in the green hue.

"Don't touch that!" Dad yells, with a grin,
As puppy gnaws on a shiny tin.
Mom sighs and points to the mess on the floor,
Those little paws, can we love them more?

Tinsel's a nightmare, it sticks everywhere,
Even to Cousin Tim, who's still in his chair.
Between tangled strings, laughter does soar,
In this festive chaos, we always want more.

So here's to the green, and all things bright,
To family, to laughter, on this merry night.
With boughs so cozy, and hearts so warm,
We'll make it through, through every charm.

Sweets of Memory's Embrace

Cookies lined up, all frosted with care,
Chocolate chips peek from the sweet, soft layer.
Little fingers sneak, oh what a bind,
The cookie jar's left with crumbs behind.

"Did you eat them?" Mom asks with a glare,
"Not me!" we shout, "I swear, I swear!"
But flour on faces and laughter abound,
The sweet smell of trouble is all around.

Candy canes hung, with a fragile swing,
The kids race in, ready to spring.
Whispers of sugar and secrets collide,
In this festive kitchen, where giggles reside.

So raise up your glasses, to sweets and delight,
To memories made on this very night.
With laughter and treats, and a sprinkle of cheer,
These moments we cherish, year after year.

Frosty Serenades

Outside it's chilly, the snowflakes dance,
We put on our mittens, join in the prance.
With snowmen standing, each with a hat,
We sing frosty tunes, while our noses go flat.

Jumping in snowdrifts, who can resist?
A snowball fight breaks, just like a twist.
The dog joins in, his wiggles a spree,
"Throw it to me!" he barks, full of glee.

Cold cheeks and laughter, the warmth we create,
With hot chocolate breaks, we can hardly wait.
A toast in the snow, to our frosty parade,
As footsies get tangled, who's up for charades?

So gather round, where the warmth fills the air,
In frostbitten laughter, none can compare.
With serenades sung, in this winter land,
We hold to each other, forever hand in hand.

Frost-kissed Sing-Alongs

Snowflakes dance on the stairs,
My hot cocoa's got marshmallow flares.
Jingle bells play a quick tune,
While I trip over my dog named Moon.

Singing loudly out of key,
The neighbors all stare at me.
Off-key carols fill the air,
As I'm stuck in a festive chair.

A tree with ornaments galore,
We're so tangled up, we can't explore.
Elves in the attic having a ball,
While I gain five pounds from cookies and all.

So let us sing and laugh in cheer,
With Frosty's hat and holiday beer.
In joyous chaos, we will find,
The merriest moments—oh, so unrefined!

Tales of Yuletide Warmth

Grandma's cookies, oh what a treat,
They may be burnt, but still taste sweet.
Uncle Joe danced by the fire,
In a plaid suit that's rather dire.

The carolers come, all out of tune,
While my cat gobbles the string from a balloon.
A reindeer costume for my pet,
They say it's cute, but I regret.

Mistletoe hangs, I dodge the kiss,
With a face like this, I can't take that risk!
Family feuds burst into laughter,
We'll tell these tales long after.

So pour the eggnog, make it flow,
Through tangled lights that flicker and glow.
With warmth in our hearts, we'll sing along,
And treasure these tales all season long!

Melodies Beneath the Stars

Under the sky, the stars shine bright,
As we roast marshmallows late in the night.
The fire crackles, we hum silly songs,
While someone's off-key, where it belongs.

Sipping cider from cups mismatched,
A raccoon comes, but it's too far attached.
Dashing through snow, we tumble and fall,
In a heap of giggles, we're having a ball.

The moon winks down, oh what a sight,
My hat's too small, it's a comical fright.
With friends by my side, cheer fills the air,
As we create memories, beyond compare.

So let's gather round in the cool evening air,
With songs and stories, we'll banish despair.
Beneath the stars, let laughter ignite,
In the warmth of our friendship, all feels right.

Scented Tales by the Fire

The fireplace crackles with scent so sweet,
While cookies bake, oh what a treat!
A cat curled up, on my favorite chair,
She yawns and stretches, without a care.

Pumpkin pie's cooling, it smells divine,
Dad sneaks a piece—oh, that'll be fine!
The dog's underfoot, begging for snacks,
While Grandma recounts her wild, holiday hacks.

With ribbons and bows, we wrap up the gifts,
Uncle Fred sighs when he spills the mints.
We gather 'round with laughter and cheer,
As the stories unfold, our love draws near.

So here's to the laughter, the warmth, and the fun,
Where every odd tale brings us more than one.
By the fire so bright, we'll share heartfelt dreams,
In this season of joy, or so it seems!

Hearthside Harmonies

The fire crackles, oh so bright,
Singing songs that warm the night.
Grandpa's snoring, such a sound,
More like a bear that's rolling 'round.

Marshmallows dance in flames so high,
Oh, where'd my eyebrows fly?
Hot cocoa spills on Grandma's dress,
We all just love this cozy mess.

Cats are plotting next to the heat,
Eyeing the turkey, what a treat!
Uncle Joe, with all his cheer,
Thinks he's a chef, but we just fear.

As we gather, laughs ignite,
Hearthside fun feels just so right.
With silly games and loud retorts,
A joyful chaos, laughter supports.

The Sweet Aroma of December

Baking cookies, such a bliss,
But wait, what's that? A small abyss!
Flour flies as joy spreads wide,
The dog sneaks in, hopes we abide.

Cinnamon swirls in the air so sweet,
But who knew dough could be a treat?
Mom's frantic dance around the house,
While Dad's just trying to shush the mouse.

Pine trees smell like fresh-cut joy,
While kids dash 'round with a giant toy.
Wrapping gifts, oh what a sight,
Have we wrapped the cat? It's quite a fright!

In December's chill, we find delight,
A season of laughter, oh what a sight.
With every smell and every cheer,
We spread the warmth, year after year.

Festive Echoes in Frost

Snowflakes fall, a blanket white,
The snowman dreams of taking flight.
But wait, there's Dad—a big old fool,
Attempting to sled down the pool!

Gifts are wrapped with too much tape,
Guess I should have helped—oh drape!
Socks are missing, shoes don't match,
Should I wear sandals? What a catch!

Christmas carols, off-key with glee,
Neighborhood folks beg us to flee.
We sing loud, with holiday cheer,
Best performance of the year!

In frosty air, we shout and play,
Echoes of laughter lead the way.
With every slip and every fall,
We celebrate, together, after all.

Warmth in the Chill

Chili bubbling on the stove,
Try not to spill when we move!
On the couch, we all collide,
Popcorn flies, it's quite the ride.

Scarves and mittens, layers galore,
It's winter, but who keeps score?
Dad claims he's tough, the king of cold,
But he's the first to fold!

Hot pies cooling on the sill,
Watch out, don't eat 'em with a thrill!
They say it's hot, but like we care?
Mouths on fire, dinner rare!

Through frozen scenes and winds that bite,
We find our way, it feels so right.
In every laugh and shared delight,
Our warmth outshines the winter's night.

Charmed by Cocoa's Embrace

In a mug so round and stout,
Cocoa bubbles with a shout.
Marshmallows dive and float,
While I sip and feel remote.

Chocolate stains on my cheeks,
Warming up my frosty peaks.
Sipping slow, not a care,
Who needs snow? I've got flair!

A sprinkle of joy, a dash of hope,
With every sip, I learn to cope.
Cocoa hugs, oh what a thrill,
Makes winter's chill taste like a mill.

So here's to cocoa, my dear friend,
This warm embrace will never end.
Forget the diet, take a chance!
In cocoa's charm, we all can dance!

Fireside Tales and Sweetened Breaths

Gather 'round the crackling flames,
Telling stories with silly names.
The smoke dances with a grin,
While marshmallows roast, let the fun begin!

Granny's ghost told jokes, quite sly,
While Uncle Bob let out a sigh.
"Back in my day, we had no phones!"
"Your stories are old!" we snapped like bones.

The cat jumped up, stole my seat!
I chased him off — now that's defeat!
But the laughs keep coming, we're all in stitches,
'Til someone spills the hot cocoa, and oh, the hitches!

Underneath the stars so bright,
Fireside tales bring pure delight.
With sweetened breaths and laughter's cheer,
Winter's gone, long live our year!

Melodies Upon a Wintry Breeze

In the cold, the night does sing,
Songs of snowflakes and winter's fling.
A cheerful tune, a frosty beat,
With jingle bells and chilly feet.

The wind whispers secrets, hushed and low,
Tickling trees with a frosty glow.
While squirrels dance on branches bare,
I laugh aloud, "Do you care?"

Snowmen strut with a carrot nose,
While icicles dangle like frozen toes.
The melody swirls, a wintery blend,
With snowflakes laughing, they never end!

So let's hum along as we trudge through the snow,
With melodies bright in the frosty glow.
Joyful and free, we dance on this breeze,
With hearts all aglow, we're sure to please!

Comfort in the Twinkling Quiet

At night, the stars put on a show,
A twinkling quilt, what a glow!
All is calm, all is bright,
Wrapped in dreams, holding tight.

Listening close, the world takes pause,
Into the silence, my mind draws.
Whispers of snowflakes touch my nose,
Nature's blanket, soft it glows.

Here I find my cozy nook,
With a good book, and a happy look.
The clock ticks slow, time slides away,
In quiet comfort, I choose to stay.

So let the twinkling lights shine clear,
Inviting all warmth, spreading cheer.
In this serene, peaceful delight,
I find my joy in the twinkling night!

The Flavor of Togetherness

When life gives you lemons, make a pie,
With a side of laughter, don't be shy.
Mix up the giggles, and sprinkle some cheer,
Together we feast, our friends always near.

In a pot of friendship, toss in some zest,
Stir up the fun, 'cause we are the best.
Add a dash of craziness, a pinch of glee,
Taste the flavor of us, just you wait and see.

From donuts to veggies, we nibble it all,
The more, the merrier, we'll never stall.
Grab a fork, twirl spaghetti with flair,
Together we savor, no need for despair.

So raise your forks high, let's toast to our crew,
Each laugh is a topping; oh, how we grew!
In this buffet of life, with flavors so bright,
Together is better, in every bite.

Hidden Wonders of the Season

Underneath the snow, there's magic to find,
Squirrels in jackets, oh so well-designed.
Glimmers of laughter, hidden in trees,
Pine cones dancing, with a gentle breeze.

In the chill of the air, the snowmen parade,
Wearing carrots like hats, they've got it made.
Snowball fights brew, as giggles arise,
Even the icicles wear funny ties.

With hot cocoa sipped, marshmallows afloat,
Watch the mugs wobble, a slippery boat.
The season hides wonders, in frost's soft embrace,
A time for delight, in this snowy place.

Let's seek the wonders, our laughter in tow,
With mudboots that squish; away we go!
In each flake that falls, let's find joy anew,
Hidden wonders await, for me and for you.

Dusted with Delightful Harmony

In the land of socks, mismatched and bold,
Dance like no one's watching, let stories unfold.
The dishes all pile, but we'll sing and we'll sway,
Life dusted with laughter, comes what may.

Tangles of fairy lights, wrapped round the dog,
She barks out a tune; such a whimsical fog.
Caught in delightful chaos, we grin ear to ear,
Every tangled moment, we hold oh so dear.

Cookies in the oven, burnt yet divine,
We'll toast to the sweetness, raise glasses of wine.
Flour on our noses, the kitchen's a sight,
In harmony's melody, we'll dance through the night.

So here's to the mess, the giggles and gripes,
To dust bunnies lurking, and laughable types.
Together in chaos, our hearts all aglow,
Dusted with harmony, let the good times flow.

Enchanted Evenings of Warmth

As nighttime whispers, and stars start to twinkle,
A cozy blanket fort, where giggles sprinkle.
We roast marshmallows, tell tales that delight,
As shadows dance happily, in flickering light.

With cocoa so creamy, and whipped cream galore,
The more we sip, the more we explore.
Jump scares from stories, we squeal with surprise,
In this enchanting night, joy never dies.

The clock ticks away, but we're lost in the fun,
Jokes fly like fireflies, and we never run.
Even the popcorn is bouncing with glee,
Each kernel a laugh, oh, the revelry!

So let's cherish the evenings, wrapped snug and tight,
With hearts full of warmth, and faces alight.
In the magic of moments, our spirits will lift,
Enchanted together, each laugh is a gift.

Catching Glances of Joy

I saw a cat wear fancy shoes,
With a swagger so bold, it made the news.
Chasing shadows, it danced with flair,
Oh, the giggles we shared, floating in air.

A squirrel in a hat, my new best friend,
Nibbled on acorns, oh, the fun won't end.
We planned a party with cookies and cake,
While doing the cha-cha, for goodness' sake!

The sun was a grin, the clouds played along,
Making silly faces, they sang us a song.
Laughter erupted, like bubbles in stew,
In the land of joy, where dreams come true.

So here's to those moments, so fleeting and bright,
When catching glances of joy feels just right.
With laughter and love, let the antics ensue,
For in this silly dance, it's always just me and you.

Fireside Conversations

In the glow of the fire, we roast marshmallows,
Sharing tales of adventure with goofy fellows.
The s'mores are sticky, but the laughter is sweet,
As we try to out-stories our uninvited heat.

A raccoon comes in, with a top hat so grand,
He joins in our fun, as we all make a band.
Playing spoons, pots, and the old tin can,
Dancing with shadows, while cracking a plan.

The flames crackle loud, telling jokes of their own,
While we ponder if cheese is better than scone.
A debate erupts on the best pizza place,
And we end up in fits, a laugh-tastic race.

In fireside conversations, we warmly embrace,
The joy of connection, a warm, silly space.
With a wink and a grin, may the laughter just grow,
In the glow of our stories, let hilarity flow.

Sugar-Plum Serenades

In the land of sweet dreams, the sugar-plums play,
They dance on the clouds, in a whimsical way.
With twirls and swirls, they sprinkle some cheer,
Oh, what a symphony, all creatures draw near!

A cookie jumps high, with a gingerbread hat,
Singing lyrics so funny, to the chubby old cat.
He winks with his whiskers, then starts a round,
Of sugar-plum serenades, laughter abounds!

A donut, so jolly, spins tales full of sprinkles,
While dancing to rhythms that cozy hearts crinkles.
The jellybeans giggle, and jelly rolls too,
As they sway in the moonlight, just like they do.

So join in the fun, let your laughter resound,
With every sweet serenade, pure joy can be found.
In the dances of sugar, and playful delight,
We'll carry the magic into the night.

A Symphony of Flavors

In a busy kitchen, the spices do meet,
A symphony of flavors, oh what a treat!
The garlic's a maestro, with onions in tow,
Creating sweet melodies, putting on a show.

The tomatoes start jamming, like a rock 'n' roll band,
While the basil keeps dancing, all green and well-planned.

Oregano strums on the pots and the pans,
Making sure all the flavors can join in the dance!

A sprinkle of salt adds the high note so sharp,
While cinnamon swirls like a sweet lullaby harp.
And as we all gather, our plates piled so high,
We feast on the music, with giggles and pie.

So here's to the kitchen, and all of its songs,
Where flavors collide, and fun surely belongs.
Together we savor, with laughter and cheer,
A symphony of flavors, we hold oh so dear.

The Taste of Homecoming

Returning home is such a treat,
With mom's cooking, can't be beat.
I search the fridge, I start to roam,
Spoilers: It's all but a stale scone.

The cookies weigh more than my backpack,
I can't resist; I'm on a snack attack.
Mom says just one, I can't comply,
Two scoops, three pies—oh me, oh my!

The taste of love, it's truly clear,
With every bite, I shed a tear.
Soggy pizza from last week's party,
Still, I laugh; it's a feast so hearty!

Home, sweet home—where calories bloom,
I'll eat till I burst in this cozy room.
Diabetes? Nah, not in my plan,
Just bring on the cake; I'm your biggest fan!

Silhouettes Against the Glow

In the night, we dance and sway,
Under stars, our feet at play.
Shadows laugh against the light,
Silly moves, what a sight!

My uncle thinks he's still so cool,
Shows off moves from some old school.
But then he trips and takes a fall,
The dance floor greets him, yes, quite the brawl!

We twirl and spin, our faces aglow,
Making fun of each other, oh what a show!
Mom's on the sidelines with popcorn in hand,
Wishing she'd join us, to take the stand.

Yet there's laughter in every silhouette,
With all this fun, there's no regret.
Under the glow, life's a grand scheme,
Just silly dances and a sweet dream!

Tinsel, Tidings, and Sweetness

Tinsel drapes like shimmering dread,
Decorating the chaos we spread.
Candy canes litter the floor like snow,
And some were eaten, I just thought you'd know!

The dog wears a hat, looking quite bold,
Trying to steal the cookies, if truth be told.
We chase him 'round, it's a merry old race,
With icing-dusted giggles all over the place!

Mom's baking pies, the oven's aglow,
Too many tastes; where do we go?
Between the stuffing and the gingerbread,
I think I'll burst; oh, where's my bed?

In happy chaos, laughter we greet,
With tinsel, tidings, and sweets to eat.
As if the calories could be undone,
In this funny holiday, we're all having fun!

A Playlist of Winter's Whimsy

Winter songs on full blast,
Jingle bells ringing, oh what a blast!
My shrug suggests I've heard them before,
But dance like nobody's watching—oh, what a score!

Snowflakes drift like confetti from skies,
But my nose is red as I yawn and sigh.
Will it ever stop? Not any time soon,
Look out, I'm stuck—oh, here comes the moon!

Hot cocoa spills in my mittens' embrace,
Sipping sweet warmth, oh, what a race!
Do I share with the snowmen I've made?
Is that a marshmallow I just decayed?

So here's my playlist, quite goofy, I text,
With winter whimsy, I'll never feel vexed.
Laughing and singing, it's all such delight,
With snowflakes twirling, let's dance into night!

Nocturnal Songs of Comfort

The moon sings softly to the trees,
Crickets chirp like they've had a few bees.
Owls hoot cautiously, sharing the news,
While stars giggle, hiding in their blue shoes.

Blankets snore, all warm and snug,
Teddy bears tap dance, giving a shrug.
Nightlights flicker a tipsy glow,
As dreams line up for the comfort show.

Mice hold concerts, all squeaky and sweet,
Dancing on table tops, shuffling their feet.
Midnight snacks haunt the hungry and brave,
As pillows whisper secrets they crave.

So snuggle up tight, don't let dreams roam,
In the dark, we find our cozy home.
With laughter and silliness all around,
Nocturnal joys, in slumber abound.

Cradling the Season's Spirit

Pumpkins giggle, all orange and round,
While leaves do the cha-cha on the ground.
Sweaters grumble, tangled in fright,
As ghosts float by, in the flickering light.

Cider bubbles, it's a warm spicy treat,
While marshmallows dance, thinking they're sweet.
The wind starts humming a jolly old tune,
To the beat of the rustling, beneath the full moon.

Squirrels chatter, their nests all a-clutter,
Collecting acorns with a cheerful flutter.
The cold nips gently, a playful tease,
As we bundle up, with such cozy ease.

So grab a warm drink, and cozy up tight,
Embrace all the quirkiness of this night.
For every season holds joy in its song,
Cradling spirits, where we all belong.

Songs of Sugar and Spice

Gingersnaps dance, all crispy and bright,
With sugar sprinkles, a magical sight.
Cinnamon swirls join in the parade,
As cakes and pies join the sweet charade.

Frosting whispers secrets, all creamy and sweet,
While cookies giggle with each crunchy beat.
A sprinkle of laughter, joy on the rise,
In the kitchen chaos, where wonder flies.

Candies play hide and seek in the jars,
A sugar rush leading to dreams of stars.
Marshmallows giggle, soft puffs of delight,
Inviting mischief into the night.

So bake with a smile, let the kitchen hum,
With songs of sweetness, the best is yet to come.
For every bite's a memory we chase,
In this sugary world, we find our place.

Echoes of a Joyful Hearth

The fire crackles, a merry old song,
As shadows dance, where we all belong.
Wooden chairs sway, with warm apple spice,
While laughter pops like rice in a nice.

Grandma tells stories, all twisty and fun,
Of goblins and fairies, and races to run.
The cat rolls its eyes, on a stack of warm quilts,
While kids trade candy, with delightful tilts.

Hot cocoa bubbles in mugs held with glee,
Toasting marshmallows, a sweet jubilee.
Stockings are hung, all ready to cheer,
As echoes of joy fill the atmosphere.

So gather around, let the good times ignite,
With friends and with family, warmth feels just right.
For in the heart's hearth, memories blend,
In this joyful echo, the laughter won't end.

The Rhythm of Joyful Eves

At dusk we dance, oh what a sight,
With socks mismatched, we twirl and bite.
A cat joins in, gives us a fright,
As we groove under the twinkling light.

The music's loud, our voices too,
We sing off-key, but keep it true.
A pizza rolls, in the oven, woo!
We'll feast on slices 'til we're blue.

With every laugh, we share the cheer,
Tomorrow's woes seem far and near.
Each joyful eve, our hearts we steer,
To treasure moments year after year.

So let's make merry, sway a bit,
In clumsy rhythm, let's not quit.
A joyful eve, where laughter's lit,
Together dancing, no need to split.

Candlelit Whispers and Scented Dreams

Amidst the glow of flickering light,
We chat like squirrels, so full of fright.
The cake is burnt, but what a sight,
With icing battles, we take a bite.

The scent of cookies fills the room,
"Oh dear!" I yell, "What's that? A broom?"
The dog is chasing, causing a gloom,
While we just laugh, a sweet perfume.

We whisper secrets, oh such a tease,
Recalling moments that never freeze.
With every giggle, we feel the breeze,
And dreams take flight, if you please.

With candles lit, our hearts do gleam,
In the chaos, we form a team.
These scented dreams don't burst the seam,
Together, always, a shared meme.

Embraced by Spiced Delight

In the kitchen, we stir with flair,
A pinch of laughter, spice in the air.
Cookies crumble, they seem unfair,
But we keep baking, with love to spare.

Pumpkin pies tease, with crust so fine,
We argue over who's had more wine.
"Just one more slice!" I draw the line,
Yet somehow, it still feels divine.

With gingerbread men, we sneak a bite,
Dressed up in frosting, oh what a sight!
We munch and crunch 'til the night is bright,
In moments of joy, everything's right.

This spiced delight warms every heart,
In the chaos, we play our part.
So let's bake on, let's make a start,
Together, forever, hand in hand, we chart.

The Frosted Song of Togetherness

In winter's chill, we bundle tight,
With frosted mugs, spirits ignite.
A snowman wobbles, what a fright,
But laughter echoes through the night.

We sing of snow, of joy, of cheer,
As flakes keep falling, we persevere.
Each cup of cocoa, every smear,
Reminds us life's better when friends are near.

The fire crackles, stories unfold,
With marshmallows sticky, young and old.
Each tale retold, like treasures of gold,
Create a warmth, against the cold.

Together we find our hearts aligned,
In frosted songs, our joys entwined.
For every moment, truly well-defined,
Is found in laughter, the sweetest kind.

Lullabies of the Holiday Glow

In the fridge, a turkey's chill,
Dreams of stuffing, oh what a thrill!
Gingerbread men with smiles so wide,
Watch them mysteriously slide!

Tinsel fights with branches above,
Santa's lost his left glove!
Mistletoe hangs, but oh what a test,
Just avoid the cousin, if you want to rest!

Grandma's snoring, a festive tune,
A carol from the bathroom, oh what a boon!
Cookies vanish, like magic tricks,
Not my fault—blame the reindeer flicks!

Night creeps in with laughter and cheer,
As we reminisce over last year's beer.
The holiday glow warms every heart,
With love and laughter, we're never apart.

Dances in the Candlelight

Candle flickers in the dark,
Watch the cat chase the spark!
Twinkle lights sing a tune,
Baking cookies that taste like a swoon!

Socks upon the floor, a sight,
Dancing 'round them, what a flight!
Uncle Joe breaks out in song,
With all the rhythm, it can't be wrong!

The punch bowl spills, what a mess,
Everyone laughs—nothing less!
Snowflakes tap at the window pane,
While we laugh at Joe's silly refrain!

Whirling crowns of festive glee,
Careful now, don't bump the tree!
With every dance, the night grows bright,
In this chaos, what pure delight!

Spiced Wishes on a Snowy Eve

Hot cocoa spills, oh what a sight,
With marshmallows floating, pure delight!
Snowflakes tumble, a frosty show,
While we dream of the gifts that glow!

Ginger snaps make a crispy crunch,
As we munch and munch and munch!
The snowman's looking a little punk,
With buttons missing and a lopsided trunk!

Shovels battle with a squeaky sound,
While the dog rolls in snow, feet off the ground!
A snowball flies, oh dear, oh no!
Straight at dad—what a cool throw!

Warm fires crackle, shadows play,
In this winter wonderland of gay!
Spiced wishes twirl through the night,
Sparking joy, oh what a sight!

The Yuletide Sonnet

A tree adorned, with baubles bright,
Yet one cheeky cat made a fright!
Tinsel glistens, a shiny game,
While we yell, "Oh cat! What a shame!"

The stockings hang, lopsided so,
Filled with trinkets, humor does flow!
With every gift wrapped tight with care,
Uncle Bob insists he won't share!

We sing loud, with off-key vibes,
While sneaking bites of pumpkin pies!
The moon peeks in, a sneaky glance,
As we laugh and twirl in this silly dance!

In this season, love conquers all,
Even the ones at the holiday brawl!
Warm hugs and laughter make spirits bright,
In this crazy, joyful, festive night!

Whispers of Winter Nights

The snowflakes dance like crazy bees,
As icy winds play hide and seek with trees.
Hot cocoa's warmth spills down my chin,
And my dog thinks he can fly, with a silly spin.

Frosty breath makes dragons puff with might,
While polar bears practice their ballet at night.
I slip on ice, a graceful disaster,
Who knew penguins were such skilled masters?

Chilly air makes everyone sneeze,
And car tires spin like we're on top of cheese.
Wrapped up snug, like a burrito I lay,
Dreaming of summer, oh please, come my way!

But winter nights bring laughter and cheer,
With cocoa mustaches, let's raise a beer!
Let's toast to cold toes and hot fireplace,
Happy winter times, in this frozen space!

Melodies in Fragrant Air

Baking cookies with flour on my face,
The dog thinks it's snow, oh what a disgrace!
Mixing spices like a mad scientist,
Get ready for a feast, I insist!

Each bubbling pot sings a silly song,
While the cat rolls sushi, yes, that's where it's wrong.
Scent of garlic wafts, oh what a delight,
But careful, my friend, the chili's a fright!

Cinnamon here, and nutmeg there,
It's a sweet-smelling chaos filling the air.
With giggles and spills, we create our mess,
Who knew cooking could be so absurdly blessed?

So let's dance with the spoons, and sing out loud,
Serve up some joy, make the neighbors proud!
In the fragrant air, our laughter is clear,
Sharing these moments, we've nothing to fear.

The Spice of Joyful Echoes

Oh, the sound of laughter, a peppery hue,
Like spices that tickle and bubble right through.
Remember those moments when joy hits the fan?
The dance of my cat in a gourmet pan!

Friends gather 'round, their stories so bold,
Each tale seasoned with a pinch of gold.
The kitchen's a stage, the spatula the wand,
Watch out for the cake, it's totally blonde!

Chili peppers spark like fireworks bright,
As friends trade slapstick, each jest a delight.
The joy of connect, so spicy and sweet,
Brings warmth to our hearts, oh what a treat!

So sprinkle some giggles and serve a loud cheer,
With laughter as goodies, we'll feast on the here!
In this banquet of life, there's never a rue,
Let's spice up our days, just me and you!

Songs Wrapped in Warmth

Wrapped in blankets, it's storytime whimsy,
The fireplace crackles, our voices get flimsy.
With ghosts in the tales and laughter that roars,
My cat's glaring at me, for opening the doors!

Each fable we spin, a melody sweet,
We dance 'round the room with our mismatched feet.
The thermostat's broken, it's getting quite warm,
But who needs a sweater with friend's silly charm?

The kettle sings songs of steam-filled delight,
While marshmallows swirl, oh what a sight!
We giggle and thump, as the music goes on,
When we sing out loud, every worry is gone.

So let's raise a cup, to the tales that we weave,
In the warmth of friendship, we all can believe.
With songs wrapped in joy, and laughter in sight,
Here's to moments that sparkle, oh what a night!

Verses of the Hearth

The fire crackles, logs in a dance,
A marshmallow launched, oh what a chance!
We laugh and we joke, in this cozy embrace,
But the cat just rolls eyes, with a glare on its face.

The kettle whistles, tea's brewing hot,
Someone spilled cocoa, now there's a blot.
Grandpa tells stories, they seem quite absurd,
About a lost sock and a very big bird.

The dog steals the cookies, oh what a scene,
He thinks it's all fair, he's the kitchen king!
We can't help but giggle, too sweet to be mad,
As he munches away, looking blissfully glad.

So let's raise our mugs, let our laughter ring,
In the warmth of the hearth, we find our zing.
May every gathering bring joy to our hearts,
With marshmallow rumbles and silliness that starts.

Frostbitten Fantasies

Outside it's frosty, snowflakes on parade,
Inside we concoct, a warm lemonade.
A snowman is built, but it looks like a blob,
With carrots for eyes, and a scarf made of sob.

Sledding on hills, we zoom down with glee,
Until someone hits a tree—oh me, oh me!
We tumble and giggle, with snow in our hair,
And icy cold fingers, but we just don't care.

Hot chocolate's a must, with marshmallows afloat,
A sprinkle of laughter, and we're all in a boat.
Dreaming of summer, while freezing our toes,
We wish for a tropical wind that just blows.

So bring on the ice, we'll embrace every chill,
With frosted fantasies and wintertime thrill.
Let's toast to the cold, and to warmth all around,
For laughter and friendship are wonderfully found.

The Warmth of Gathering

Friends all around for a feast that we share,
But oh! Where's the turkey? It's lost in mid-air!
The table is set, but there's just one big plate,
We're laughing too hard, should we just wait?

The salad's all leafy, tossed in a bowl,
While Uncle Joe's story just starts to unroll.
It's wild and it's wacky, but wait, is that true?
The dog barks in laughter, enjoying the stew.

A toast to the moments, let the fun never cease,
Raising our glasses, we savor the peace.
In comfort and joy, our hearts swell and sing,
As we gather together, and let the laughs ring.

So here's to the gatherings, so hearty, so bright,
Our homes filled with laughter, oh what a delight!
With bowls full of stories, and hearts that are light,
Let's cherish these moments, both silly and right.

Sweetened Reflections Beneath the Stars

We sit by the fire, reflections aglow,
Each star twinkles down, with a wink and a show.
The night air is crisp, with a hint of sweet pie,
As we share silly jokes, and dreams that fly high.

A raccoon peeks in, searching for snacks,
While we hide the cookies, keeping all tracks.
But laughter bursts forth, as he scurries away,
Leaving us grinning, and shouting hooray!

Ghost stories emerge from the depths of our minds,
Transforming our friends into spooks of all kinds.
Though they jump and they holler, soon laughter prevails,

As we chant spooky tales about ghostly snails.

So here's to the nights spent beneath starlit skies,
With friends that are cherished, and gobbling up pies.
In sweetened reflections, our hearts beat as one,
For under the stars, this sweet laughter's begun.

Milton Keynes UK
Ingram Content Group UK Ltd.
UKHW022123091224
452185UK00010B/469